Holy Bible Poetry

Popular Biblical Passages in Rhyme

Holy Bible Poetry

Popular Biblical Passages in Rhyme

Copyright © 2018 by Gary W. Parker

All rights reserved.

This book or any part thereof may not be reproduced without written consent of the publisher.

Published in the United States by Gary W. Parker.

ISBN: 9781796615746

Contents

Revised Standard is the version of each Biblical passage, unless noted with (KJV) for the King James Version.

Biblical Passage (Version)	Poem Title	Page
List of All Old Testament Books (no. of poems from each)		x
List of All New Testament Books (no. of poems from each)		xi
Preface		xiii
Old Testament Poems		1
Genesis 1: 1-2 (KJV)	In the Beginning	3
Genesis 1: 28	Be Fruitful and Multiply	4
Genesis 2: 7	God Formed Man	5
Genesis 2: 21-2	God Made Woman	6
Exodus 15: 1-13	The Song of Moses	7
Exodus 33: 14	Give You Rest	11
Numbers 6: 24-26	Benediction I	12
Deuteronomy 6: 5-7	Great Commandment	13
Deuteronomy 10: 12-13	What God Requires	15
Deuteronomy 28: 1-2	Blessings of Obedience	16
Deuteronomy 32: 1-4	Second Song of Moses	17
Joshua 1: 9	God Is With You	19
Ruth 1: 16	Ruth's Devotion	20
1 Samuel 2: 1-10	Hannah's Prayer	21
1 Samuel 16: 7	Look On the Heart	25
1 Chronicles 16: 8-15	Psalm of Thanksgiving I	26

Biblical Passage (Version)	Poem Title	Page
1 Chronicles 16: 23-27	Psalm of Thanksgiving II	28
1 Chronicles 16: 30-34	Psalm of Thanksgiving III	29
1 Chronicles 16; 35-36	Psalm of Thanksgiving IV	31
1 Chronicles 29: 10-13	David's Prayer	32
Job 1: 21	Blessed Be the Lord	34
Psalm 1: 1-2	Law of the Lord	35
Psalm 8: 1-2	Majestic Is Thy Name	36
Psalm 16: 11	Path of Life	37
Psalm 18: 1-3	Lord Is My Rock	38
Psalm 19: 7-8	Messages of the Lord	39
Psalm 19: 9	Fear and Ordinances	40
Psalm 23 (KJV)	The Lord Is My Shepherd	41
Psalm 25: 1-2	Lift Up My Soul	43
Psalm 27: 1 (KJV)	Whom Shall I Fear?	44
Psalm 28: 7	The Lord Is My Strength	45
Psalm 29: 2 (KJV)	Give Unto the Lord	46
Psalm 34: 4 (KJV)	Seek the Lord	47
Psalm 37: 7	Be Still and Wait	48
Psalm 40: 1-3	Trust in the Lord I	49
Psalm 41: 1-2	He Who Considers the Poor	50
Psalm 46: 1	Refuge and Strength	51
Psalm 46: 10	Be Still and Know	52
Psalm 55: 22	Cast Your Burden	53
Psalm 69: 30	Praise and Magnify	54
Psalm 74: 21-22	Poor and Needy	55
Psalm 84: 1-2	Lovely Is Thy Dwelling Place	56
Psalm 89: 1-2	Thy Steadfast Love I	57
Psalm 90: 14	Thy Steadfast Love II	58
Psalm 92: 1-3	Give Thanks to the Lord	59
Psalm 95: 1-2 (KJV)	Let Us Sing	60

Biblical Passage (Version)	Poem Title	Page
Psalm 95: 1-3	Joyful Noise	61
Psalm 100	Praise and Thanksgiving	62
Psalm 106: 1	Praise the Lord	63
Psalm 118: 24	This Is the Day I	64
Psalm 118: 24	This Is the Day II	65
Psalm 119: 105	Lamp to My Feet	66
Psalm 121: 1-2	Help from the Lord	67
Proverbs 1: 8-9	Parental Teaching	68
Proverbs 2: 6-8	Lord Gives Wisdom	69
Proverbs 3: 5-6	Trust in the Lord II	70
Proverbs 6: 20-23	A Lamp and a Light	71
Proverbs 28: 13	Obtain Mercy	72
Proverbs 31: 10-12	Good Wife	73
Ecclesiastes 3: 1-8 (KJV)	Time For Every Purpose	74
Ecclesiastes 3: 14	God Made It So	76
Ecclesiastes 11: 1-2	Cast Your Bread	77
Ecclesiastes 12: 13	Duty of Man	78
Isaiah 7: 14	The Lord's Sign	79
Isaiah 9: 6-7 (KJV)	The Prince of Peace	80
Isaiah 12: 2	God Is My Salvation	82
Isaiah 40: 31	Wait For the Lord	83
Isaiah 42: 10	New Song	84
Isaiah 43: 5	I Am With You	85
Isaiah 56: 1-2	Do Righteousness	86
Jeremiah 17: 7-8	Trust in the Lord III	87
Jeremiah 17: 14	Thou Art My Praise	88
Lamentations 3: 22-23	Love of the Lord	89
Ezekiel 36: 26-27	A New Heart	90
Daniel 2: 20-23	Daniel's Thanks to God	91
Hosea 6: 1-3	Know the Lord	93

Biblical Passage (Version)	Poem Title	Page
Hosea 12: 6 (KJV)	Wait On Thy God	94
Joel 2: 12-13	Return to the Lord	95
Jonah 2: 2-9	Jonah's Prayer	96
Micah 6: 8	Walk Humbly With God	98
Nahum 1: 7	The Lord Is Good	99
Zephaniah 3: 17	Victory Warrior	100
Zechariah 7: 9-10	Word of the Lord	101
Zechariah 8: 16-17	Things You Shall Do	102
New Testament Poems		103
Matthew 3: 11 (KJV)	He That Cometh	105
Matthew 3: 16-17 (KJV)	My Beloved Son	106
Matthew 5: 3-10	The Beatitudes	107
Matthew 6: 9-13 (KJV)	The Lord's Prayer	110
Matthew 7: 1-3	Judge Not	112
Matthew 7: 7-8	Ask, Seek and Knock	113
Matthew 10: 27	Utter in the Light	114
Matthew 10: 39	Find Your Life	115
Matthew 11: 28 (KJV)	Come Unto Me	116
Matthew 12: 18-21	Justice to Gentiles	117
Matthew 12: 25	Divided Against Itself	119
Matthew 13: 3-9	Parable of the Sower	120
Matthew 13: 31-32	Mustard Seed Parable	122
Matthew 16: 18	The Rock	124
Matthew 16: 24-27	Come After Me	125
Matthew 17: 20	Grain of Mustard Seed	127
Matthew 18: 20	Gather In My Name	128
Matthew 19: 4-6	Two Shall Become One	129
Matthew 21: 22	Pray With Faith	130
Matthew 22: 37	Love the Lord	131

Biblical Passage (Version)	Poem Title	Page
Matthew 23: 11-12	Your Servant	132
Mark 3: 35	Will of God	133
Mark 6: 4	A Prophet's Honor	134
Mark 10: 13-15	Let the Children Come	135
Mark 11: 24	Pray With Belief	137
Luke 1: 30-33	Mary's Favor with God	138
Luke 1: 46-53	The Magnificat	140
Luke 2: 6-11 (KJV)	Birth of Jesus	142
Luke 2: 14 (KJV)	Glory to God	144
Luke 6: 27-29	Love Your Enemies	145
Luke 8: 18	Him Who Has	146
Luke 11: 23	Not With Me	147
Luke 17: 21	Kingdom of God	148
Luke 21: 25-28 (KJV)	Signs of the End	150
John 1: 12-13	Children of God	151
John 3: 6-7	Born Anew	152
John 3: 16	Eternal Life	153
John 4: 36	Sower and Reaper	154
John 8: 31-32 (KJV)	Truth Make You Free	155
John 10: 9-11	The Good Shepherd	156
John 11: 25	Resurrection and the Life	157
John 14: 6 (KJV)	Way, Truth and Life	158
John 14: 27	Peace I Give To You	159
John 15: 12-13	Golden Rule	160
Acts 2: 17	Last Days	161
Acts 7: 49-50	Heaven Is My Throne	162
Acts 17: 24-25	Lord of Heaven and Earth	163
Acts 17: 28	In Him We Live	164
Romans 3: 23-25	All Have Sinned	165
Romans 8: 28 (KJV)	All Things For Good	166

Biblical Passage (Version)	Poem Title	Page
Romans 8: 31-32	Who Is Against Us?	167
Romans 8: 38-39	Nothing Will Separate Us	168
Romans 10: 9-10	You Will Be Saved	169
Romans 12: 2	Renewal of Your Mind	170
Romans 12: 9-13	Conduct	171
Romans 13: 1 (KJV)	No Power But Of God	173
Romans 15: 21	Never Heard of Him	174
1 Corinthians 2: 9	What God Has Prepared	175
1 Corinthians 13: 1-3	Have Not Love	176
1 Corinthians 13: 4-8	Love Never Ends	178
1 Corinthians 13: 11	Childish Ways	180
1 Corinthians 13: 13	Love Is the Greatest	181
1 Corinthians 15: 55	Death's Victory	182
2 Corinthians 5: 17	In Christ	183
2 Corinthians 13: 14	Benediction II	184
Galatians 5: 14	One Word	185
Galatians 6: 7-10	Sow to the Spirit	186
Ephesians 5: 14	Christ Shall Give You Light	188
Philippians 4: 13 (KJV)	All Things Through Christ	189
Colossians 1: 15-20	God's Beloved Son	190
1 Thessalonians 5: 2	Coming of the Lord	191
1 Timothy 3: 16	Mystery of Our Religion	192
1 Timothy 4: 4-5	God Is Good	193
1 Timothy 6: 6-10	Root of All Evils	194
2 Timothy 1: 7 (KJV)	Spirit of Fear	196
Titus 3: 1-2	Reminders	197
Titus 3: 5-7	Mercy and Grace	198
Hebrews 10: 16	The Covenant	199
Hebrews 11: 1-3	The Nature of Faith	200

Biblical Passage (Version)	Poem Title	Page
Hebrews 12: 1	Run with Perseverance	201
Hebrews 12: 5-6	Discipline of the Lord	202
Hebrews 12: 14	Strive For Peace	204
James 2: 14	Faith Without Works	205
1 Peter 3: 10-12	Eyes and Face of the Lord	206
2 Peter 3: 8-9	A Thousand Years	207
1 John 2: 4-6	Keep His Word	208
1 John 2: 9-10	In the Light	209
1 John 4: 18	No Fear in Love	210
Revelation 1: 3	The Time is Near	211
Revelation 3: 20	Open the Door	212
Revelation 15: 3-4	King of the Ages	213
Revelation 21: 3-4	Death Shall Be No More	214

Revised Standard is the version of each Biblical passage, unless noted with (KJV) for the King James Version.

THE NAMES AND ORDER

OF ALL THE 39

BOOKS OF THE OLD TESTAMENT

WITH THE NUMBER OF POEMS FROM EACH

Genesis	4	*Ecclesiastes*	4
Exodus	2	*Song of Solomon*	
Leviticus		*Isaiah*	7
Numbers	1	*Jeremiah*	2
Deuteronomy	4	*Lamentations*	1
Joshua	1	*Ezekiel*	1
Judges		*Daniel*	1
Ruth	1	*Hosea*	2
1 Samuel	2	*Joel*	1
2 Samuel		*Amos*	
1 Kings		*Obadiah*	
2 Kings		*Jonah*	1
1 Chronicles	5	*Micah*	1
2 Chronicles		*Nahum*	1
Ezra		*Habakkuk*	
Nehemiah		*Zephaniah*	1
Esther		*Haggai*	
Job	1	*Zechariah*	2
Psalms	32	*Malachi*	
Proverbs	6		

THE NAMES AND ORDER

OF ALL THE 27

BOOKS OF THE NEW TESTAMENT

WITH THE NUMBER OF POEMS FROM EACH

Matthew	21	1 Timothy	3
Mark	4	2 Timothy	1
Luke	9	Titus	2
John	10	Philemon	
Acts	4	Hebrews	5
Romans	9	James	1
1 Corinthians	6	1 Peter	1
2 Corinthians	2	2 Peter	1
Galatians	2	1 John	3
Ephesians	1	2 John	
Philippians	1	3 John	
Colossians	1	Jude	
1 Thessalonians	1	Revelation	4
2 Thessalonians			

Preface

I am not a biblical scholar or religion expert, but like Christians and Jews everywhere, I enjoy reading and believe in the messages and lessons in popular Biblical passages.

One of my favorite passages is St. Paul's beautiful, definitive description of "love" found in *1 Corinthians 13: 4-8*. For years I wondered if it might be even more popular and maybe a more effective learning tool or reference source if there was an additional version that was a rhyming poem with consistent timing and meter rather than a narrative.

I decided to see if I could transform it into poetry by adding a few like-messaged rhyming words and phrases while retaining the actual passage itself in its entirety. To my pleasant surprise, with the help of God given analytic and artistic aptitudes and listening to my inner voice additional words and phrases emerged into my consciousness to accomplish this objective without, at least to my mind, detracting from or destroying the original message. In fact, for me the message was clarified or enhanced to some degree.

With this satisfying personal success it occurred to me that other popular verses might lend themselves to similar poetic transformations, so without realizing it at the time, an enjoyable and inspirational project and mission was initiated.

Each poem included herein incorporates a complete Biblical passage, every word in order including punctuation. Nothing from the original verses is excluded. The ***italicized, bold print*** is the actual passage from the Bible, so it can be read by itself for review or comparison.

As few message consistent words and phrases as necessary are inserted in and around each passage to produce a rhyming poem with consistent meter. The additional words are intended, or at least hoped, to clarify or enhance the passage's message as well.

The Biblical verses are primarily from the Revised Standard Version (RSV), although some are from the King James Version (KJV). The choice was based on which version seemed more popular to me or would lend itself more easily to the poetic transformation.

Most of the credit for these poems should go to the divinely inspired authors of books in the Holy Bible. It is of course much easier to make additions and supplement than it is to write the original text from scratch.

It is hoped this poetic approach may attract larger adult, and especially youth, audiences to the timeless lessons in the greatest book ever written. Perhaps reading and reflecting on God's word in this format will trigger new insight, learning and inspiration for you as well as you read each Bible verse poem.

You may want to read the book slowly so you have time to ponder and revalidate your understanding of each passage and its message. As you read each poem listen to your inner voice for new thoughts, ideas and even principles for you to consider adopting and incorporating into your values, your behavior and ultimately who you are.

Editor

For love transcends and ***never ends.***
1 Corinthians 13: 8

Old Testament Poems

In the Beginning   *(Genesis 1: 1-2 (KJV))*

1. In the beginning God created the heaven and the earth,

Originating the universe, a miraculous birth.

2. And the earth was without form, was inhospitable **and void;**

In God's evolutionary plan more was to be deployed,

And darkness was everywhere **upon the face of the deep**,

And the world seemed to be in a continuous nighttime sleep.

And the spirit of God moved upon the face of the waters,

And the earth was made ready for his future sons and daughters.

Be Fruitful and Multiply *(Genesis 1: 28)*

And God blessed them, and God said to them, "This is how you do it.

Be fruitful and multiply, and fill the earth and subdue it;

And have respectful *dominion over the fish in the sea*

And over the birds of the air and the creatures that roam free

And over every living thing that moves upon the earth",

Each animal created for them to utilize its worth.

God Formed Man   *(Genesis 2: 7)*

Then the Lord God formed man of dust from the ground

In his own image from the loose dirt he found**,**

And breathed into his nostrils the breath of life,

The volume of air filling his lungs was rife**;**

And at once **man became a living being.**

Man's evolution God was overseeing.

God Made Woman   *(Genesis 2: 21-24)*

21. So the Lord God caused a deep sleep to fall upon the man to refresh**,**

And while he slept God ***took one of his ribs and closed up its place with flesh;***

22. And the one ***rib which the Lord God had taken from the man*** while asleep

He formed and ***made into a woman and brought her to the man*** to keep.

23. Then the man said,

"This at last is the ***bone of my bones and flesh of my flesh*** and my clan***;***

She shall be praised and ***called Woman, because she was taken out of Man."***

24. Therefore a man leaves his father and his mother and cleaves to his wife,

And they become one flesh and they love and support each other for life**.**

The Song of Moses *(Exodus 15: 1-13)*

1. …"I will sing out **to the Lord, for he has triumphed gloriously;**

The horse and his rider he has deceived and **thrown into the sea.**

2. The Lord is my strength, my protector **and** the subject of **my song,**

And he has become my salvation for he is righteous and strong**;**

This is my God, and I will praise him, when I needed him he came.

3. The Lord is a man of war for his people**; the Lord is his name.**

4. Pharaoh's strongest **chariots and his host he cast into the sea;**

And his picked officers are sunk in the Red Sea trying to flee.

5. *The floods cover them*, engulf and rush over them like a cyclone;

They were lost and ***went down into the depths*** of the ***sea like a stone.***

6. *Thy right hand, O Lord,* is ***glorious in power*** and great in might,

Thy right hand, O Lord, shatters the enemy so he cannot fight.

7. *In the* brute strength of thy hand and the ***greatness of thy majesty***

Thou dost ***overthrowest thy adversaries*** for their travesty;

Thou sendest forth thy worst ***fury,*** and ***it consumes them like stubble.***

8. *At the blast of thy nostrils the waters piled up* to cause trouble,

The rushing ***floods stood up*** and crashed ***in a heap*** on the enemy;

The deeps congealed and surrounded Pharaoh ***in the heart of the sea.***

9. The enemy said, 'I will pursue, I will overtake and maul,

I will divide the spoil, my desire shall have its fill of them all.

I will draw out *my sword,* and *my hand shall destroy*, crush and pound *them.*'

10. Thou didst blow a storm **with thy wind,** and **the sea covered** and drowned **them;**

They sank to the depths of the sea **as lead in the mighty waters.**

11. Who is like thee, O Lord, among the gods, who judges and slaughters?

Who is like thee, majestic in holiness, who plots and plunders,

Terrible in glorious deeds, doing miraculous **wonders?**

12. ***Thou didst*** look out over the enemy and ***stretch out thy right hand,***

The earth and the sea opened and ***swallowed them*** just as thou had planned***.***

13. ***Thou hast led in thy steadfast love the people whom thou hast redeemed,***

Thou hast guided them by thy strength to thy holy abode long dreamed***.***

Give You Rest *(Exodus 33: 14)*

And Moses sought to be led,

So t*he* Lord to Moses ***said,***

"My presence will go with you,

So you will know what to do.

You will be forever blest,

And I will give you your ***rest."***

Benediction I   *(Numbers 6: 24-26)*

24. The Lord bless you and keep you away from strife*:*

      25. The Lord make his face to shine once **upon you,**

Love you **and be gracious to you** and your wife*:*

      26. The Lord lift up his countenance upon you,

And give you peace and harmony all your life*.*

Great Commandment *(Deuteronomy 6: 5-7)*

5. And you shall love the Lord your God with all of *your heart,*

And with all your soul, and with all your might as a start.

6. And these words which I command and consign *you this day*

Shall be indelibly etched *upon your heart* to stay;

7. And you shall teach them diligently to your children

In the same way God taught them to you as a pilgrim,

And shall talk of and prize ***them when you sit in your house***

With your family, guests and especially your spouse,

And when you gather with your friends and ***walk by the way,***

And when you lie down, and when you rise every day.

What God Requires *(Deuteronomy 10: 12-13)*

12.** ...So now I ask of you, **what does the Lord your God require of you,

What does he expect of you and what should you then desire to do,

But to fear the Lord your God, to walk in all** of **his ways, to love him,

To honor and praise him and worship no other gods above him,

To serve the Lord your God with all your heart and with all your soul,

To release control of your life to him as your singular goal,

13. And to keep the commandments and statutes of the Lord** as you should**,

Which I** now communicate and **command you this day for your good?

Blessings of Obedience *(Deuteronomy 28: 1-2)*

1. And if you obey the voice of the Lord your God who is without flaws,

Being careful to do all of ***his commandments*** and follow his laws

Which I command you this day to value your life and honor your birth,

The Lord your God will set you high above all the nations of the earth.

2. And all these blessings will come upon you, surround ***and overtake you,***

If you obey the voice of the Lord your God who will not forsake you.

Second Song of Moses *(Deuteronomy 32: 1-4)*

*1. "**Give ear** to my voice, **O heavens, and I will speak** now;*

And let the earth hear the truth in the *words of my mouth.*

*2. May my teaching drop as the rain*drops fall to renew,

And may *my speech distil* broadly *as the* morning *dew,*

*As the gentle rain*s *upon the tender grass* nourish,

And as the showers upon the herb garden flourish.

3. For I will proclaim the name of the Lord with high praise.

Ascribe greatness to our God throughout all of my days!

4. The Rock, his work is perfect and is forever true;

For all of ***his ways are*** based on grace and ***justice***, too.

A God of faithfulness and without iniquity,

Just and right is he now as throughout antiquity."

God Is With You   *(Joshua 1: 9)*

Have I not charged and *commanded you*

To obey the law I handed you*?*

Always *be strong and of good courage*,

For the Lord will never discourage*;*

Be not frightened, neither be dismayed;

Keep your faith, so you are never swayed,

For the Lord your God, you should now know,

Is with you wherever you may *go.*

Ruth's Devotion   *(Ruth 1: 16)*

...**"Entreat me** I pray **not to leave you**,

Retreat like I do not believe you

Or to return from following you

Or to refrain from shadowing, too;

For wherever **you go I will go,**

And whatever you sew I will sew.

What enemy you dodge I will dodge,

And wherever **you lodge I will lodge;**

For **your people shall be my people,**

Your church steeple shall be my steeple.

I shall follow you where you have trod,

And I vow **your God** shall be **my God;"**

Hannah's Prayer   *(1 Samuel 2: 1-10)*

1. ..."My heart exults and rejoices *in the Lord:*

My strength is exalted in the Lord's reward.

My mouth derides my enemies' elation,

Because I can *rejoice in thy salvation.*

2. There is none holy like the Lord is holy,

There is none besides thee who loves the lowly;

*There is no*t a *rock like our God* is a rock,

Who preserves and protects and defends his flock.

3. Talk no more so very proudly or sorely,

Let not arrogance come from your mouth toward me;

For the Lord is a God of knowledge self-made,

And by him actions are created and *weighed.*

4. The bows of the mighty are broken and shed,

5. Those who were full have hired themselves out for bread,

But those who were hungry have ceased to hunger,

Each stomach being filled by a bread monger.

The barren has borne seven just as was sworn,

But she who has many children is forlorn.

6. The Lord kills and brings to the barren new **life;**

He brings down to Sheol and raises up a wife,

7. The Lord makes poor and makes rich though they have faults;

He brings rivals **low,** and **he also exalts.**

8. He raises up the poor from the dusty deep;

And **he lifts** up **the needy from the ash heap,**

To make them sit with princes, nobles and queens,

And inherit a seat of honor and means.

For the pillars of the earth are the Lord's own,

And on them he has set the world cornerstone.

9. *He will guard the feet of his* most *faithful ones*,

Paving the pathways for his daughters and sons;

But the wicked shall be cut off in darkness

And the afflicted cured of being heartless;

For not by might shall a man win or ***prevail.***

A man's might versus the Lord is bound to fail.

10. *The* misguided *adversaries of the Lord*

Shall be broken* into *pieces by his sword;

Against them he will bring ***thunder on heaven.***

His wrath is swift and not designed to leaven.

The Lord will judge man to ***the ends of the earth***

To evaluate his value and his worth;

He will give strength to his king once appointed,

And exalt the power of his anointed."

Look On the Heart   *(1 Samuel 16: 7)*

*"...**For the Lord** God **sees not as man sees***

When ascertaining good qualities*;*

Man looks on the outward appearance

For his superficial adherence**,**

***But the Lord** God **looks** first **on the heart"**,*

For the heart is where wisdom will start.

Psalm of Thanksgiving I *(1 Chronicles 16: 8-15)*

8. O give thanks to the Lord, call on his holy name,

Make known his deeds among the peoples and exclaim!

9. Sing to him, sing praises to him all of your days,

Tell of all his wonderful works and wondrous ways!

10. Glory in his holy name with persistent voice;

Let the hearts of all *those who seek the Lord rejoice!*

11. Seek out *the Lord and his strength* habitually,

Seek his presence and guidance *continually!*

12. Remember the wonderful works that he has done,

Remember his power that is second to none,

The wonders he wrought, and ***the judgments he uttered,***

The sinners he sought when their lives were left cluttered,

13. O offspring of Abraham his faithful ***servant,***

Sons of Jacob, his chosen ones, true and fervent***!***

14. He is the Lord our God who grants us our lives and worth;

His judgments are just and righteous ***in all the earth.***

15. He is mindful of his covenant for ever,

Of the word that he commanded we not sever***,***

May it live on ***for a thousand generations,***

Providing peace and harmony to all nations.

Psalm of Thanksgiving II *(1 Chron. 16: 23-27)*

23. Sing praises **to the Lord,** for **all the earth** we pray**!**

Tell of his grace and **salvation from day to day.**

24. Declare his glory among the nations' steeples**,**

His marvelous works among all of **the peoples!**

25. For great is the Lord, and greatly to be praised,

And grace is the Lord's, his wonder to be raised,

And he is to be held in awe above all gods,

Saving us from our transgressions above all odds**.**

26. For all the false **gods of the peoples are idols;**

But the Lord made the heavens, his love unbridles**.**

27. Honor and majesty are before him to brace**;**

Strength and joy are pervasive **in his** holy **place.**

Psalm of Thanksgiving III *(1 Chron. 16: 30-34)*

30. Let us all **worship the Lord in holy array;**

Tremble before him, and **all the earth** will obey;

Yea, the world stands firm, its stance **never to be moved.**

Yet the Lord can affirm, his strength never disproved.

31. Let the heavens be glad, and let the earth rejoice,

For the Lord speaks to those who listen for his voice,

And let them say among the nations, "The Lord reigns!"

32. Let the sea roar, and all that fills its hurricanes,

Let the field exult, and everything in it!

33. Then shall the trees of the wood sing for joy's minute

Before the Lord, for he comes then *to judge the earth*

And to evaluate each individual's worth.

34. O give thanks to the Lord, for he is good and just;

For his steadfast love endures for ever for us!

Psalm of Thanksgiving IV *(1 Chron. 16: 35-36)*

*35. ...So: "Deliver us O God of our salvation*s,

And gather and save us from among the nations,

That we may give thanks and praise *to thy holy name,*

And glory in thy praise of the highest acclaim.

36. Now *blessed be the Lord, the God of Israel,*

From everlasting to everlasting as well"!

David's Prayer *(1 Chronicles 29: 10-13)*

10. ..."*Blessed art thou, O Lord, the God of Israel* we all share,

Our father, who *for ever and ever* will always be there.

11. *Thine, O Lord, is the greatness, and the* raw *power* that is true,

And the glory, and the victory, and the majesty, too;

For all that is conceived *in the heavens and the earth is thine;*

Thine is the kingdom, O Lord, all thy creations are divine,

And thou are exalted as head above all of life to be.

12. *Both riches and honor come* solely and completely ***from thee,***

And thou rulest over all the peoples as their guiding light.

In thy hand are immense ***power and*** immeasurable ***might;***

And in thy hand it is to make great things and break down each wall,

To grant peace and joy to believers ***and to give strength to all.***

13. And now we thank thee, O God, and we praise thee with high acclaim,

We give thanks for thy love and grace, ***and praise thy glorious name.***

Blessed Be the Lord   *(Job 1: 21)*

...***"Naked I came from my mother's womb*** to learn**,**

And at my life's end ***naked shall I return;***

The Lord gave, and the Lord has taken away;

Still ***blessed be the name of the Lord*** I say***."***

Law of the Lord   (Psalm 1: 1-2)

1. ***Blessed is the man who walks*** unafflicted,

   Not in the evil ***counsel of the wicked,***

   ***Nor stands in the way of sinners*'** vain offers,

   Nor sits in the derisive ***seat of scoffers;***

2. ***But his delight is in the law of the Lord,***

   His commitment to God is its own reward,

   And on his law he meditates day and night.

   He lives his life to illuminate God's light.

Majestic Is Thy Name   *(Psalm 8: 1-2)*

1. O Lord, our Lord, who watches over us from birth,

How majestic is thy name in all of *the earth!*

Thou whose glory above the heavens is chanted

*2. By the mouth*s *of babes and infants* thee implanted*,*

Thou hast founded a bulwark because of thy foes,

To still the enemy and the avenger's woes.

Path of Life *(Psalm 16: 11)*

***Thou dost show me the path of life** to employ;*

***In thy presence there is fullness of** great **joy**,*

***In thy right hand are pleasures for evermore**,*

And in thy light are mercy and grace galore.

The Lord Is My Rock   *(Psalm 18: 1-3)*

1. I love thee, O Lord, my strength; calm the fears of a shiverer.

2. The Lord is my rock, and my fortress, and my deliverer,

My God, my rock, in whom I take refuge from distress and cold,

My shield and the horn of my salvation, my sword and *stronghold.*

3. I call upon the Lord, who alone *is worthy to be praised,*

And I am saved from my enemies, my righteousness unphased.

Messages of the Lord   *(Psalm 19: 7-8)*

*7. **The law of the Lord is** a **perfect** goal,*

Reviving** and enlivening **the soul;

The testimony of the Lord is sure,

***Making wise the simple** to feel secure;*

*8. **The precepts of the Lord are** just and **right,***

***Rejoicing the heart** and giving it flight;*

The** clear **commandment of the Lord is pure,

***Enlightening the eyes**, God's truths endure.*

Fear and Ordinances   *(Psalm 19: 9)*

The fear of the Lord is clean** to pursue**,

*****Enduring for ever** like the weather**;*****

The ordinances of the Lord are true,

*****Eternal *and righteous altogether.******

The Lord Is My Shepherd   *(Psalm 23 (KJV))*

1. **The Lord is my shepherd** and guide;

   I shall not want and cannot hide**.**

2. **He maketh me** want **to lie down**

   In green pastures where peace is found**:**

   He leadeth me gently **beside**

   The still waters where truths reside**.**

   Though life mistakes may take their toll,

3. **He restoreth my** broken **soul:**

   He leadeth me in the path'**s** make

   Of righteousness for his name's sake.

4. **Yea, though I walk through the valley**

   Of the shadow of death's alley**,**

   I will fear no evil: for thou art with me;

   Thy rod and thy staff they will **comfort**eth **me.**

5. ***Thou preparest a table before me***

In the presence of all *mine enemies:*

Thou anointest my head with oil;

My cup runneth over *with spoil.*

6. ***Surely goodness and mercy*** flow

        Through all of my struggles and strife;

They ***shall follow me***, this I know,

        For ***all*** of ***the days of my life:***

And I will dwell with God together

In the house of the Lord forever.

Lift Up My Soul   *(Psalm 25: 1-2)*

1. *To thee, O Lord, I* pray you **lift up my soul.**

2. *O my God, in thee I trust* and know my role,

   Let me not be put to shame improperly;

   Let not my enemies exult over me.

Whom Shall I Fear? *(Psalm 27: 1 (KJV))*

The Lord is my light and my salvation;

Whom shall I fear and what subjugation*?*

The Lord is the strength and rock *of my life;*

Of whom shall I be afraid and what strife*?*

The Lord Is My Strength *(Psalm 28: 7)*

***The Lord is** both **my strength and my shield**,*

And my sword is the Lord's sword to wield;

***In him my heart trusts** for good results;*

I am helped, and** how **my heart exults,

And with my song I give thanks to him

For the peace I have received through him.

Give Unto the Lord   *(Psalm 29: 2 (KJV))*

Give unto the Lord the glory

Due unto his name's only-ness;

Worship the Lord's sacred story

In the beauty of holiness.

Seek the Lord   *(Psalm 34: 4 (KJV))*

I once ***sought the Lord, and he heard me,***

My life was restored as he spurred me

And delivered me from all my fears,

Calming my heart and drying my tears.

Be Still and Wait *(Psalm 37: 7)*

When anxiety has soared,

Be* ye *still before the Lord,

And wait patiently for him;

Fret not yourself over him

Who* now *prospers in his way,

And earns profits as he may,

Over the man who carries

Against his adversaries

Out* his *evil devices

Causing consequent crisis***!***

Trust in the Lord I *(Psalm 40: 1-3)*

1. *I* have *waited patiently for the Lord;*

He inclined to me and heard me cry hard.

2. *He drew me up from the desolate pit,*

Out of the miry bog and muddy grit,

And set my feet firmly *upon a rock,*

Making my steps secure as if to lock.

3. *He put a new song in my mouth* to laud,

A song of glorious *praise to our God.*

Many righteous *will see*, believe *and fear,*

And put their trust in the Lord to adhere.

He Who Considers the Poor *(Psalm 41: 1-2)*

1. Now ***blessed is he*** forever more;

He is one ***who considers the poor!***

The Lord delivers to ***him*** double

In the darkest ***day of*** his ***trouble;***

2. The Lord protects him so he will thrive,

And keeps him healthy, free and ***alive;***

He is called blessed in all ***the land;***

And will always be held in God's hand.

Refuge and Strength   *(Psalm 46: 1)*

God alone ***is our refuge and strength***

Throughout all of eternity's length,

A very present help in trouble,

Whether it be minor or double.

Be Still and Know *(Psalm 46: 10)*

Be still* for the full impact,*

And know this truth is intact

That I, who have never lacked,

Am God and that is a fact.

Cast Your Burden   *(Psalm 55: 22)*

Cast your burden on the Lord, and he will sustain you;

He will not allow strife to destroy or detain you;

Have faith in God and his support of you will be proved,

For ***he will never permit the righteous to be moved.***

Praise and Magnify *(Psalm 69: 30)*

I will praise the name of God with a song;

I will sing his praises all the day long;

I will magnify him with thanksgiving,

And lift his name each day I am living**.**

Poor and Needy   *(Psalm 74: 21-22)*

*21. **Let not the downtrodden be put to shame;***

Let the poor and** the **needy praise thy name.

*22. **Arise, O God, plead thy cause** steadfastly;*

Remember how the impious scoff at thee...!

Lovely Is Thy Dwelling Place   *(Psalm 84: 1-2)*

1. ***How lovely is thy dwelling place,***

   O Lord of hosts, our God of grace***!***

   2. ***My*** weary ***soul longs,*** and ***yea, faints***

   For the courts of the Lord and saints***;***

   My heart and flesh sing and applaud

   For pure ***joy to the living God.***

Thy Steadfast Love I *(Psalm 89: 1-2)*

*1. **I will sing** with grateful praise **of thy steadfast love, O Lord, for ever;***

> ***With my mouth I will proclaim thy faithfulness to all generations.***

*2. **For thy steadfast love was established for ever** that none can sever,*

> ***Thy faithfulness is firm as the heavens*** and proclaimed to all nations.

Thy Steadfast Love II   *(Psalm 90: 14)*

Satisfy us in the morning

With thy steadfast love adorning*,*

That we may rejoice in high praise

And be saved and *glad all our days.*

Give Thanks to the Lord   *(Psalm 92: 1-3)*

1. *It is good to give thanks to the Lord,* I vie

To sing great *praises to thy name, O Most High;*

2. *To declare thy steadfast love in the morning,*

And thy faithfulness by night, my heart warming

3. *To the* sweet *music of the lute and the harp,*

To the melody of the lyre, clear and sharp.

Let Us Sing *(Psalm 95: 1-2 (KJV))*

1. ***O come, let us sing*** a grand chord

   Of sweet music ***unto the Lord:***

   Let us all ***make a joyful noise***,

   Children's choirs of both girls and boys,

   To the rock of our salvation

   And the source of all creation.

   So as we sing our last encore,

2. ***Let*** each one of ***us come before***

   His presence with our ***thanksgiving,***

   With our gratitude based living,

   And make a joyful noise, no qualms,

   As we sing ***unto him with psalms.***

Joyful Noise   *(Psalm 95: 1-3)*

*1. **O come, let us sing to the Lord***, the fount of all creation*;*

Let us make a joyful noise to the rock of our salvation!

*2. **Let us come into his presence with thanksgiving**'s chords ablaze;*

Let us make a joyful noise to him with *grateful songs of praise!*

*3. **For the Lord***, our redeemer and sustainer, **is a great God,***

And a great King above all gods *who hide in a false facade.*

Praise and Thanksgiving *(Psalm 100)*

1. Make a joyful noise to the Lord, all the lands' church bells are ringing*!*

2. Serve the Lord with gladness! And *come into his presence with singing!*

3. Know that the Lord is God! It is he that made us in his stature,

And we are his; we are his people, and the sheep of his pasture.

4. Enter his gates with thanksgiving, and honor *his courts with* high *praise!*

Give thanks to him, and humbly *bless his* holy *name* all of your days*!*

5. For the Lord is good and just*; his steadfast love endures for ever,*

And his faithfulness he grants *to all generations* together.

Praise the Lord   *(Psalm 106: 1)*

Praise the Lord and honor his fatherhood*!*

O give thanks to the Lord, for he is good;

For his steadfast love endures for ever!

His grace he grants to righteous endeavor.

This Is the Day I *(Psalm 118: 24)*

This is the day which the Lord has made,

A wondrous way his love is displayed;

Let us rejoice and be glad in it.

Let us enjoy each blessed minute.

This Is the Day II *(Psalm 118: 24)*

Come and shout, "Hooray!"

For ***this is the day***

Which the Lord has made;

His wonder displayed.

So ***let us rejoice***

By raising each voice

In praise each minute

And be glad in it.

Lamp to My Feet   *(Psalm 119: 105)*

Thy word is a lamp to my feet,

A plan and roadmap to repeat,

A reference guide for my days,

And a light to my path always***.***

Help from the Lord   *(Psalm 121: 1-2)*

1. Now *I lift up my eyes*

To the hills and the skies.

From whence does my help come?

Must I fight for each crumb?

Not from the club or sword,

2. *My help comes from the Lord,*

Who made heaven and earth,

And fills my heart with mirth.

Parental Teaching *(Proverbs 1: 8-9)*

8. Hear, my son, your father's instruction and preaching***,***

And reject not your mother's counsel and ***teaching;***

9. For they are a fair garland for your head's knowledge***,***

And pendants for your neck, your parental college***.***

Lord Gives Wisdom   (Proverbs 2: 6-8)

6. For the Lord gives wisdom that is ever expanding;

From his mouth come sacred **knowledge and understanding;**

7. He stores up sound wisdom for the upright's verity;

He is a shield to those who walk in integrity,

8. Guarding the paths of justice for wisdom achievers

And preserving the way of his saints and believers.

Trust in the Lord II   *(Proverbs 3: 5-6)*

5. Trust in the Lord with all your heart and might**,**

And **do not rely on your own insight.**

6. In all your ways acknowledge him with praise**,**

And he will make straight your paths and byways**.**

A Lamp and a Light   (Proverbs 6: 20-23)

20. My son, keep your father's commandment, his edict your rule,

And forsake not your mother's teaching, her wisdom your tool.

21. Bind them closely and securely **upon your heart always;**

Tie them about your neck and live by them throughout your days.

22. When you walk, they will lead you and guide you with perfect sight;

When you lie down, they will watch over you throughout the night;

And when you awake, they will talk with you with great insight.

23. For the commandment is a lamp and the teaching a light....

Obtain Mercy   *(Proverbs 28: 13)*

***He who conceals his transgressions** and sin*

Will not prosper** or ultimately win**,

But he who confesses and forsakes them

Will obtain** God's **mercy** as he shakes them**.

Good Wife   *(Proverbs 31: 10-12)*

10. A good wife who can find? She is far more precious than jewels.

11. The heart of her husband trusts in her to follow God's rules,

And he will have no lack of gain for he has a good wife.

12. She does him good, and not harm, all of **the days of her life.**

Time For Every Purpose   *(Eccl. 3: 1-8 (KJV))*

1. To every thing and for every person ***there is a season,***

And a time for every purpose under the heaven to reason*:*

2. A time to be born, and a time to die, life not taken for granted*;*

A time to plant, and a time to pluck up all of ***that which is planted;***

3. A rarely justified ***time to kill, and a time to*** repent and ***heal;***

A time to break down, and a time to build up your confidence and zeal*;*

4. A time to feel sadness and ***weep, and a time to laugh*** and take a chance*;*

A time to regret and ***mourn, and a time to*** be lighthearted and ***dance;***

5. *A time to cast away stones, and a time to gather stones together;*

A time to embrace, and a time to refrain from embracing ever;

6. *A time to get* everything that you deserve**, *and a time to lose;***

A time to keep, and a time to cast away all that you cannot use;

7. *A time to rend* or tear apart ***and a time to*** reconnect and ***sew;***

A time to keep silence, and a time to speak of all the good you know;

8. *A time to* express your ***love, and*** when sin is exposed ***a time to hate;***

A time for war, a last resort, *and a time for peace* to celebrate.

God Made It So   *(Ecclesiastes 3: 14)*

I know for sure *that whatever God does*

Lasts and *endures for ever* as it was*;*

Nothing more *can be added to* sum *it,*

Nor can *anything* be *taken from it;*

God has made it so, not a trial or whim,

In order that men should fear before him.

Cast Your Bread *(Ecclesiastes 11: 1-2)*

1. Cast your bread upon the waters and mind your ways,

For you will surely ***find it after many days.***

2. Give a portion to seven, or even to eight,

Be generous and gracious to control your fate,

For you know not what evil may happen on earth

Or just how the Lord may evaluate your worth.

Duty of Man *(Ecclesiastes 12: 13)*

This is ***the end of the matter*** and last word*;*

All has been experienced, expressed and ***heard.***

Fear God, and keep his commandments as your plan*;*

For this is the whole truth and ***duty of man.***

The Lord's Sign   *(Isaiah 7: 14)*

Therefore, the Lord himself will give you a sign that you should not shun.

Behold, with God's help ***a young woman shall conceive and bear a son,***

And shall call his name Immanuel, for he is the chosen one.

The Prince of Peace   (Isaiah 9: 6-7 (KJV))

6. For unto us a child is born to pay the price,

Unto us a son is given in sacrifice:

And the government of all **shall be** his station

And **upon his shoulder** rests mankind's salvation:

And his name shall be called Wonderful, Counselor,

The al**mighty God, The everlasting Father,**

The Prince of Peace whose term and reign will never cease.

7. Of the increase of his government and of **peace**

There shall be no end, upon the throne of David,

And upon his kingdom which is never dated,

*To order it, and to establish it*s toughness

With sound *judgment and with* compassionate *justice*

From henceforth even for ever without deceit.

The zeal of the Lord of hosts will perform this feat.

God Is My Salvation   *(Isaiah 12: 2)*

*"**Behold, God is my salvation** for which I prayed;*

I will trust** in him**, and** I **will not be afraid;

*derp**For the Lord God is my strength and** also **my song,***

***And he has become** why **my salvation** is strong**.**"*

Wait For the Lord *(Isaiah 40: 31)*

...But they who wait for the Lord shall renew their strength,

They shall mount up with wings like eagles spread full length*,*

They shall run long distances *and not be weary,*

They shall walk and not faint when it's dark and dreary.

New Song   *(Isaiah 42: 10)*

Let us ***sing to the Lord a*** glorious ***new song,***

His praise from the end of the earth with voices strong***!***

Let the sea roar and all the water **that fills it,**

The coastlands and their inhabitants, God wills it**.**

I Am With You   *(Isaiah 43: 5)*

Fear not, for I am with you;

I will bring your offspring, too.

From the east, and from the west

I will gather you, my blessed*;*

Do Righteousness   *(Isaiah 56: 1-2)*

1. Thus says the Lord: "Keep justice, and do righteousness to have your soul healed**,**

For soon my salvation will come, and my deliverance be revealed.

2. Blessed is the man who does this, and the son of man who holds it fast,

Who keeps the Sabbath, not profaning it, repents from his sinful past,

And keeps his hand from doing any evil", his righteousness steadfast**.**

Trust in the Lord III *(Jeremiah 17: 7-8)*

7. "Blessed is the man who trusts in the Lord, whose trust is the Lord to redeem.

8. He is like a tree planted by water, that sends out its roots by the stream,

And does not fear when heat comes, for its leaves remain green from the breadth of root,

And is not anxious in the year of drought, for it does not cease to bear fruit."

Thou Art My Praise *(Jeremiah 17: 14)*

Heal me, O Lord, and I shall be healed;

Save me, and I shall be saved and sealed*;*

I will follow you all of my days

For thou art the subject of *my praise.*

Love of the Lord   *(Lamentations 3: 22-23)*

***22. The steadfast love of the Lord**, it **never ceases**,*

***His mercies never come to an end** in pieces;*

***23. They are** brand **new every morning**, noon and night;*

For **great is thy faithfulness** and bright is thy light.

A New Heart   *(Ezekiel 36: 26-27)*

26. A brand ***new heart I will give you*** for a fresh start**,**

*And a new spirit I will put within you*r heart*;*

And I will take out of your flesh the heart of stone

And give you a heart of flesh you will call your own**.**

27. *And I will put my spirit within you* to please**,**

And cause you to walk in my statutes and decrees

And be careful to observe my ordinances,

Turning away from your past impermanences**.**

Daniel's Thanks to God (Daniel 2: 20-23)

20. ..."Blessed be the name of God for ever and ever,

To whom belong wisdom and might for him to lever.

21. He changes times, weather **and** he changes the **seasons;**

He removes kings and sets up kings for the right reasons;

He gives wisdom and appreciation **to the wise**

And knowledge to those who have understanding to prize;

22. He reveals to his flock **deep and mysterious things;**

He knows what is in their hearts and what **the darkness** brings,

And the light dwells with him more than with all the others.

23. *To thee* and only to thee, ***O God of my fathers,***

I give to you my most grateful ***thanks and*** highest ***praise,***

For thou hast given me wisdom and strength to amaze,

And hast now made known to me what we all ***asked of thee,***

For thou hast made known to us the king's matter for free."

Know the Lord   *(Hosea 6: 1-3)*

1. *"Come let us* repent and let us *return to the Lord;*

   For he has torn, that he may heal us to be restored;

   He has stricken, and he will bind us up though we fuss.

2. *After two days he will* then return to *revive us;*

   On the third day he will mercifully *raise us up,*

   That we may live before him at his table to sup.

3. *Let us know, let us press on to know the Lord* we pray;

   His going forth is sure as the dawn of each new day;

   He will come to us as the life enriching *showers,*

   As the spring rains that water the earth and bring flowers."

Wait On Thy God *(Hosea 12: 6 (KJV))*

Therefore turn thou to thy God *for his grace:*

Keep mercy and *sound **judgment** as your base,*

Obey each law individually

And wait on thy God continually.

Return to the Lord   *(Joel 2: 12-13)*

12. …Repent and *"return to me* now **with all your heart,**

With fasting, with weeping, and with mourning to start;

13. Cleanse your mind **and rend your hearts and not your garments."**

Return to the Lord, your God away from torments**,**

For he is gracious and merciful from above**,**

Slow to anger, and abounding in steadfast love…

Jonah's Prayer *(Jonah 2: 2-9)*

2. "I called to the Lord from the bowels of the fish, *out of my distress,*

And fortunately *he answered me* and he agreed to reassess;

*Out of the belly of Sheol I cried, and thou didst hear my voice*d pleas.

3. For thou didst cast me into the deep, down into the heart of the seas,

And the flood was sur*round*ing me and was just *about* to cover *me;*

All thy waves and thy billows rose up and suddenly *passed over me.*

4. Then I said to the Lord, *'I am cast out* and am barred *from thy presence;*

How shall I again look upon thy holy temple's acquiescence*?'*

5. The waters closed in over me, would the world now move on without me?

It seemed that my life might be over for **the deep was round about me;**

6. Weeds were wrapped about my head at the roots of the mountains of the deep.

I went down to the land whose bars closed upon me for ever to sleep;

Yet thou didst bring up my life from the Pit, O Lord my God, with your grace.

7. When my soul fainted within me, I remembered the Lord to save face;

And my prayer came to thee, into thy holy temple's pure royalty.

8. Those who pay regard to their **vain idols forsake their true loyalty.**

9. But I with the voice of thanksgiving will sacrifice to thee my sword;

For **what I have vowed I will pay. Deliverance belongs to the Lord!**"

Walk Humbly With God *(Micah 6: 8)*

For ***he has showed you, O man, what is good***,

That you love one another as you should;

So now what does your God ask you to do

And what else ***does the Lord require of you***

But to do justice, and to love kindness,

To turn away from your sinful blindness,

And to walk humbly with your God, the Lord?

For atonement will be your just reward.

The Lord Is Good   *(Nahum 1: 7)*

The Lord is good, his strength is double,

A stronghold in the day of trouble;

He knows those who take refuge in him

From the love that has always been him.

Victory Warrior *(Zephaniah 3: 17)*

The Lord, your God, is in your midst to be blessed,

A warrior who gives victory to oppressed;

He will rejoice over you with his ***gladness,***

He will renew you in his love from sadness;

He will exult over you with loud singing

As on a day of festival bells ringing.

Word of the Lord   *(Zechariah 7: 9-10)*

9. "Thus says the Lord of hosts, for it is his word to honor one another,

Render true judgments, show loving **kindness and mercy each to his brother,**

10. Do not oppress the widow, the fatherless, the sojourner, or the poor;

And let none of you devise evil against his brother in your heart's core."

Things You Shall Do   *(Zechariah 8: 16-17)*

16. Now *"these are the things that you shall do*

Which are honorable, good and true*:*

You *speak the truth to one another,*

Love, respect and honor your brother,

Render in your gates judgments and rules

*That are true and make for peace*ful tools*,*

So now before any anger starts

17. Do not devise evil in your hearts

Against one man, *another* or both*,*

Love your neighbor *and love no false oath…"*

New Testament Poems

He That Cometh *(Matthew 3: 11 (KJV))*

So to Abraham's son or daughter,

I indeed baptize you with water

And set your path ***unto repentance***,

Release and free you from life's sentence*:*

But he that will ***cometh after me***

Is mightier than I, you will see,

Whose shoes I am not worthy to bear,

Whose cloak I would be unfit to wear*:*

He shall baptize you to lift you higher

With the Holy Ghost, and seal ***with fire.***

My Beloved Son   *(Matthew 3: 16-17 (KJV))*

The Baptist recognized who he prized,

16. And Jesus, when he was then **baptized,**

Went up straightway out of the water

To be tempted but not to totter**:**

And lo, the heavens were opened unto him,

> **And he saw the Spirit of God descending like a dove,**

Floating slowly down **and lighting upon him**,

> A pure and simple emissary of mercy and love**:**

17. And lo there came **a voice** portraying,

The voice it came **from heaven, saying,**

This is my beloved Son unseized,

My one child **in whom I am well pleased.**

The Beatitudes   *(Matthew 5: 3-10)*

So to all those who can hear it,

3. "Blessed are the poor in spirit,

Distraught and searching for safe haven,

For theirs is the kingdom of heaven.

4. Blessed are those who mourn,

Yearning to be reborn,

For they shall be comforted,

Consoled as their mothers did;

5. Blessed are the meek,

Not considered weak,

For they shall inherit the earth,

While rejoicing in their rebirth.

6. Blessed are those who hunger and thirst for righteousness,

Those who recognize and believe in God's graciousness,

For they shall be satisfied,

Never to be cast aside.

7. Blessed are the merciful,

Forgiving and versatile,

For they shall obtain mercy,

Not strife or controversy.

8. Blessed are the pure in heart,

For they are doing their part,

Deserving a nod,

For they shall see God.

9. Blessed are the peacemakers,

The brave and true risk takers,

For they shall be called sons of God

As they calm those who ride roughshod.

10. *Blessed are those who are persecuted for righteousness' sake,*

Those who may be martyred or sacrificed or burned at the stake,

For theirs is the kingdom of heaven";

Their reward is seven times seven.

The Lord's Prayer *(Matthew 6: 9-13 (KJV))*

Praying in secret will allay thee.

9. After this manner therefore pray ye:

Our Father which art in heaven,

Maker of all we are given,

Hallowed be thy holy ***name***,

Worthy of praise and high acclaim.

10. Thy kingdom come. Thy will be done,

And our final atonement won

In earth, as it is in heaven,

Our rebirth, as it is written.

11. Give us this day our daily bread.

We express our thanks for each shred,

12. And forgive us of all ***our debts,***

Trespasses, mistakes and regrets,

As we forgive** all **our debtors,

Thereby releasing our fetters.

13. And lead us not into temptation,

Avoiding guilt and separation,

But deliver us from evil,

Protecting us from upheaval:

For thine alone **is the kingdom,**

Giving us hope, joy and freedom,

And the power, and the glory,

With love and grace as the story,

And we will be together then

For ever and ever. **Amen.**

Judge Not *(Matthew 7: 1-3)*

1. "Judge not, that you be not judged, rejected or begrudged.

2. For with the judgment that you pronounce you will be judged,

The grace shown as you live will be the treasure you net,

And the measure you give will be the measure you get.

3. Why do you see the speck that is in your brother's eye,

But do not notice the log in your own bothered *eye?"*

Ask, Seek and Knock   *(Matthew 7: 7-8)*

7. "Simply **ask, and it will be given you;**

Seek and you will find his forgiveness, too;

Then **knock, and it will be opened to you;**

God will reveal what he wants you to do.

8. For every last **one who asks receives,**

And he who seeks finds what true faith achieves,

And to him who knocks it will be opened",

So ask, seek and knock to join the chosen.

Utter in the Light   *(Matthew 10: 27)*

What I tell you in the dark,

        Go and ***utter in the light;***

I reveal to you the spark,

        So now cause it to ignite.

And what you softly ***whispered,***

        Proclaim upon the housetops.

What is being ministered,

        Exclaim until your doubt stops.

Find Your Life *(Matthew 10: 39)*

***He who finds his** earthly **life will** soon **lose** and unwind **it**,*

And he who loses his life for my sake will** then **find it.

Come Unto Me *(Matthew 11: 28 (KJV))*

So you will clearly see,

Come swiftly ***unto me,***

Both you and your neighbor,

All ye that now ***labor***

And are heavy laden,

Be shepherd or maiden,

And I will give you rest

For hard work will be blessed.

Justice to Gentiles *(Matthew 12: 18-21)*

18. "Behold, my faithful *servant whom I have chosen;*

He is the Lamb of God of whom I have spoken,

My dear *beloved with whom my soul is well pleased,*

My only son whose soul cannot be harmed or seized.

I will lovingly *put my Spirit upon him;*

So the future of man will no longer be grim,

And he shall proclaim justice to all *the Gentiles,*

Saving and releasing them from troubles and trials.

19. He will not wrangle or cry aloud of great feats,

Nor will any one hear his lone *voice in the streets:*

20. He will not bend, compromise or **break a bruised reed**

Or quench a smoldering wick, or crack a small seed,

Till he brings absolute **justice to victory:**

He alone turns prophesy into history,

21. And in his name will the Gentiles hope" and believe**.**

God grants his grace and mercy for them to receive.

Divided Against Itself   (Matthew 12: 25)

Knowing their thoughts, he said to them regarding conflicts they faced,

"Every kingdom divided against itself is laid waste,

And no city or house divided against itself will stand;"

In every case the division is reduced to wasteland.

Parable of the Sower   (Matthew 13: 3-9)

3. And in his sermon ***he told them many things***

In parables, saying what the good soil brings***:***

*"**A sower went out to sow*** the seeds he hath,

4. And as he sowed, some seeds fell along the path,

And the birds came and devoured all of ***them*** found***.***

5. Other seeds fell on rocky and stone filled ***ground,***

Where they had not much soil or shade of a shrub***,***

And almost ***immediately they sprang up,***

Since they had no fertile dirt or ***depth of soil,***

6. But when the sun rose they were scorched in turmoil***;***

And since they had no root they withered away.

7. Other seeds fell upon thorns in disarray***,***

And the thorns grew up and choked them until slain.

8. Other seeds fell on good soil and brought forth grain,

Some a hundredfold, some sixty, some thirty.

9. He who has ears, let him hear of the sturdy."

Mustard Seed Parable   *(Matthew 13: 31-32)*

Now Jesus went forth to all of his disciples conveying

31. Another parable lesson **he put before them, saying,**

"The kingdom of heaven is much **like a grain of mustard seed,**

A small kernel of energy that is destined to succeed,

Which a man took out, planted and nurtured **and sowed in his field;**

32. It is the smallest of all seeds, disguising its future yield,

But when it has grown it is the greatest of shrubs all can see;

It realizes its full destiny **and becomes a tree,**

So that the birds of the air come and make nests in its branches,"

A shelter of shade and security for farms and ranches.

The Rock *(Matthew 16: 18)*

And I tell you, you will be well known,

For *you are Peter,* which means the "stone",

And on this rock I will build my church,

The final answer for mankind's search,

And the powers of death's tireless fit

Shall not win or *prevail against it.*

Come After Me   *(Matthew 16: 24-27)*

24. "If any man would decide to *come after* and shadow *me,*

Let him deny himself, and take up his cross and follow me.

25. For whoever would save his life will lose it and unwind *it,*

And whoever loses his life for my sake will then *find it.*

26. For what will it profit or benefit *a man, if he gains*

The whole world and forfeits his life in paradise where God reigns*?*

What does a man forsake and repay for his self-induced strife

Or what shall a man forfeit and *give in return for his life?*

27. ***For the Son of man*** and God's final judgment ***is*** yet ***to come***

To the anticipation, delight and atonement of some,

With all of ***the angels*** and ***in the glory of his Father,***

Which is above and beyond the glory of any other,

And then he will evaluate and ***repay every man***

For what he has done" and how he has lived throughout his life span.

Grain of Mustard Seed *(Matthew 17: 20)*

*"**For truly, I say to you,** and please take heed,*

If you have faith as a grain of mustard seed,

You will say to this mountain from top to base,

'I command you to move hence to yonder place,'

And it will move just as you told it to do;

And nothing will be impossible to you."

Gather In My Name   *(Matthew 18: 20)*

"For where two or three are gathered in my name,

There am I in the midst of them, I proclaim*."*

Two Shall Become One   *(Matthew 19: 4-6)*

4. *"Have you not read that he* alone *who made them* unveil

From the beginning made them known as *male and female,*

5. *And said, 'For this reason a man shall* from his own life

Leave his father and mother and be joined to his wife,

And the two shall become one, life together begun*?'*

6. *So they are no longer two* living apart *but one.*

What therefore God has joined as a couple *together,*

Let no man put asunder, separate or tether*."*

Pray With Faith   *(Matthew 21: 22)*

"And whatever you ask in prayer, you will receive,

***If you** truly **have faith** and sincerely believe."*

Love the Lord   *(Matthew 22: 37)*

"You shall love the Lord your God with all your heart,

The most important message I can impart,

And** then **with all your soul, and with all your mind."

Love the Lord completely and all humankind.

Your Servant *(Matthew 23: 11-12)*

11. He who is the **greatest among you shall be your servant**,

And the service provided will be selfless and fervent;

12. Whoever exalts himself will be humbled and halted**,**

And whoever humbles himself will be more **exalted.**

Will of God   (Mark 3: 35)

*"**Whoever** sheds the rod*

*And **does the will of God***

***Is** ever **my brother**,*

*And **sister, and mother.**"*

A Prophet's Honor   *(Mark 6: 4)*

*"**A prophet is not without honor** or fame,*

***Except in his own country** from whence he came,*

***And among his own kin** who may doubt or grouse,*

***And** even from family **in his own house.**"*

Let the Children Come   (Mark 10: 13-15)

Some poor mothers viewed their plight as too grim,

13. And they were bringing their **children to him,**

That he might touch, restore and **renew them;**

And some of **the disciples rebuked them.**

14. But when Jesus saw it he fled from them;

He was indignant, and he **said to them,**

"Let the children, each one a tender stem,

Come to me, do not stop or **hinder them;**

For to such belongs the kingdom of God

Where saints and angels walk on holy sod.

15. Truly, I say to you, whoever does not receive,

And who does not have faith and innocently perceive

***The kingdom of God like a child shall not enter it"**,*

And life will be adrift without faith to center it.

Pray With Belief   *(Mark 11: 24)*

"Therefore I tell you, whatever you humbly *ask in prayer,*

Believe that you will receive it, and you will, I declare."

Mary's Favor with God   (Luke 1: 30-33)

30. "…Do not be afraid, Mary, for you have found favor with God.

God is rewarding your righteousness and giving you his nod.

31. And behold, you will soon *conceive in your womb and bear a son,*

And you shall call his name Jesus, for he is the chosen one.

32. He will be great, and he *will be called the Son of the Most High;*

His life will be a truth testament worthy to glorify,

And the Lord God will give to him the throne of his father David,

A seat at God's right hand for a life that will never be dated,

33. And he will then **reign over the house of Jacob for ever;**

Securing man's relationship with God no one can sever,

And of his glory and of his **kingdom there will be no end."**

You can be sure and confident your honor God will defend.

The Magnificat   (Luke 1: 46-53)

46. And Mary said, "My soul now glorifies and **magnifies the Lord,**

47. And my spirit rejoices in God my Savior for my reward**,**

48. For he has regarded high **the low estate of his handmaiden.**

For behold, all the **generations will call me blessed**, not laden**;**

49. For he who is mighty has done great things for me, ending my shame**,**

His love and grace are immeasurable **and holy is his name.**

50. And his mercy is on those who fear him in every nation

From the current **generation to** each future **generation.**

51. He has shown strength with his arm, all powerful in all of his parts,

He has scattered the proud in the imagination of their hearts,

52. He has put down the high and ***mighty from their*** temporary ***thrones,***

And exalted those of low degree to even greater milestones;

53. He has filled the hungry with good things, a delectable array,

And the rich he has brought down to their knees and ***sent empty away.***

Birth of Jesus   (Luke 2: 6-11 (KJV))

6. And so it was Mary's time*, that, while they were there,*

The days were accomplished to bring forth God's sole heir,

That she should be delivered with the chosen one.

7. And in a stable *she brought forth her firstborn son,*

And wrapped him in swaddling clothes and cradled his head,

And laid him in a manger as a makeshift bed;

Because there was no room left *for them in the inn.*

8. And there were in the same country working therein

Shepherds abiding in the field under starlight,

Keeping protective ***watch over their flock by night.***

9. ***And, lo, the angel of the Lord came upon them,***

And the glory of the Lord shone round about them;

And they fell down to their knees and ***were sore afraid.***

10. ***And the angel*** then ***said unto them*** as they prayed***,***

Fear not: for behold, the birth of a baby boy***,***

I bring you all news and ***good tidings of great joy,***

Which shall be to all people the life, truth and way***.***

11. ***For unto you is born*** on ***this*** world changing ***day***

In the city of David a Saviour to lead***,***

Which is Christ the Lord and all of you will be freed***.***

Glory to God   *(Luke 2: 14 (KJV))*

Glory to God in the highest,

Praise to the Lord from the pious,

And on earth peace, good will toward men.

Forever and ever: Amen.

Love Your Enemies   *(Luke 6: 27-29)*

27. *...Love your enemies,* those who berate you,

Moreover **do good to those who hate you,**

28. Bless those who curse you, who hurt and use you,

Sincerely **pray for those who abuse you.**

29. Now **to him who strikes you** right **on the cheek,**

Offer the other also; softly speak,

And then **from him who takes away your coat**

Do not withhold even your shirt or tote.

Him Who Has   (Luke 8: 18)

"Take heed then how you hear and be driven;

For to him who has will more be given,

And in stark contrast from him who has not,

Even what things he thinks that he has got

Will be squandered, lost or taken away",

For his life has gone awry and astray.

Not With Me   *(Luke 11: 23)*

Now *he who is not with me*

Is against what will lift *me,*

And he who does not gather

With me scatters his lather.

Kingdom of God *(Luke 17: 21)*

…Not a distant pod,

The kingdom of God,

If you're born anew,

Is found ***within you.***

Signs of the End   (Luke 21: 25-28 (KJV))

25. And there shall be signs in the sun and Mercury to Mars,

And there will also be signs **in the moon, and in the stars;**

And upon the earth there will be **distress of** all **nations,**

With perplexity, complexity and confrontations;

The sea and the tidal **waves** will be **roaring** so severe;

26. Men's hearts will be fibrillating and **failing them for fear,**

And for looking after those things of destruction and dearth

Which are soon to be emerging and **coming on the earth:**

For the powers of heaven shall be stirred up and *shaken.*

27. *And then shall they see the Son of man* suddenly waken,

Coming in a cloud with immense *power and great glory.*

28. *And when these things begin to come to pass* in this story,

Then look up with great joy, *and lift up your heads* to the sky;

For your long sought *redemption*, it finally *draweth nigh.*

Children of God   *(John 1: 12-13)*

12. But to all who received him and his preaching**,**

Who believed in his name and in his teaching**,**

He gave his believers the **power** and love

To become chosen **children of God** above;

13. Who were born, not of blood of earthly mothers

Nor of the will of the flesh of all others

Nor of the will of any physical **man,**

But of God in accordance with his grand plan**.**

Born Anew   (John 3: 6-7)

6. "That which is born of the flesh is flesh, parents rear it,

And that which is re-**born of the Spirit is spirit.**

7. Do not question why or **marvel that I said to you,**

'You must surrender your control to **be born anew.'"**

Eternal Life   *(John 3: 16)*

Let your heart be unfurled,

For God so loved the world

That he gave his only son,

His precious begotten one,

For whom the world still grieves,

That whoever believes

In him should not perish,

His truth is to cherish;

Not be burdened with strife,

But have eternal life.

Sower and Reaper *(John 4: 36)*

Listen to this lesson for the ages:

He who reaps** and harvests **receives wages,

Feeds family, avoids financial strife,

And gathers fruit for** his **eternal life,

***So that sower and reaper** who gather*

May rejoice** and celebrate **together.

Truth Make You Free   *(John 8: 31-32(KJV))*

31. …"*If you continue in my word,*

And follow the teaching you heard,

You are truly my disciples

Who no longer worship idols**,**

32. And you will know the truth from me**,**

And lo**, the truth will make you free."**

The Good Shepherd *(John 10: 9-11)*

9. *I am the door* to salvation sharing the key;

If anyone enters the door through and ***by me,***

He will be saved and will be destined for rapture,

And he ***will go in and out and find*** green ***pasture.***

10. *The thief comes only to steal and kill and destroy;*

I came to bring my sheep still waters to enjoy;

I came that they may have life that will never cease,

And have it abundantly filled with love and peace.

11. *I am the good shepherd* sent to sow and to reap.

The good shepherd lays down his life for the lost ***sheep.***

Resurrection and the Life   *(John 11: 25)*

"I am the resurrection and the life

And I give direction away from strife;

He who believes in me I shall forgive,

Though he die in body, **yet shall he live,**

And whoever lives and believes in me

Shall never die throughout eternity."

Way, Truth and Life   *(John 14: 6 (KJV))*

While to Thomas it may have seemed grim,

So now ***Jesus saith unto him,***

I am the way, the truth and the life,

The pathway out of trouble and strife.

No man cometh unto the Father,

But by me*,* not by any other***.***

Peace I Give To You   *(John 14: 27)*

My *peace I* now *leave with you;*

My peace I now *give to you;*

Not merely *as the world gives*,

But only as the Lord lives,

Do I now *give* just *to you*,

And it will strengthen you, too.

Let all your strengths be doubled.

Let not your hearts be troubled,

Neither let them be afraid,

Anxious, concerned or dismayed.

Golden Rule *(John 15: 12-13)*

12. This is my* new *commandment for you to pursue,

That you love one another as I have loved you.

13. Greater love has no man than this love which God sends***,***

*That **a** righteous **man lay down his life for his friends.***

Last Days *(Acts 2: 17)*

And in the last days it shall be, God declares,

To recognize and answer all of your prayers,

That I will pour out my Spirit on all flesh,

To cleanse every heart and body refresh,

And your sons and your daughters shall prophesy,

Foretelling the future before it draws nigh,

And your young men shall see visions the Lord deems***,***

And your old men shall dream incredible ***dreams;***

Heaven Is My Throne (Acts 7: 49-50)

49. Heaven is my throne, and earth is my footstool.

Do I need a home to establish my rule?

What house will you build just for me, says the Lord;

What structure would suffice that you could afford**,**

Or what is the ultimate **place of my rest?**

50. Did not my hand make all these things manifest**?**

Lord of Heaven and Earth   *(Acts 17: 24-25)*

Paul spoke as his audience whirled,

24. "For God who made mankind **the world**

And everything good **in it,**

In what seemed to him a minute,

Being Lord of heaven and earth,

Providing air, water and turf,

Does not live in shrines made by man,

25. Nor is he served by human hands,

As though he still **needs anything,**

For he alone is the wellspring,

Since he himself gives all of **men,**

And women and all of their kin,

Life and health and everything,"

Maker of earth, heavenly king.

In Him We Live   *(Acts 17: 28 (KJV))*

For in him we live, and move, and have our being,

For he is our creator who is all seeing***;***

As certain also of your own poets have said,

For we are also his offspring, children he bred.

All Have Sinned   (Romans 3: 23-25)

23. Since all have sinned and fall short of the glory of God with behavior,

> **24. They are justified by his grace as a gift** to wash away their mud,

Through the redemption which is in Jesus the Christ, their Lord and savior,

> **25. Whom God put forward** to atone as an expiation by his blood...

All Things For Good   *(Romans 8: 28 (KJV))*

And we know that all things work together for good

To them that love God *and each other as they should,*

To them who are the called *and also justified*

According to his purpose *to be glorified.*

Who Is Against Us? *(Romans 8: 31-32)*

31. ...So ***if God*** himself ***is for us,***

Who is against to deplore ***us?***

32. ***He who did*** resolve ***not*** to ***spare***

And further determined to share

His own Son so not to enthrall,

But God ***gave him up for us all,***

So ***will he not also give us***

All things with him to be with us***?***

Nothing Will Separate Us *(Romans 8: 38-39)*

38. For I am quite *sure that neither death, nor life,*

Nor angels, nor principalities, nor strife,

Nor things now *present, nor things* destined *to come,*

Nor powers perceived as dominant by some*,*

39. Nor height, nor depth, nor breadth, nor deviation,

Nor anything else in all of *creation,*

Will be able to separate us, this horde,

From the love of God in Christ Jesus the Lord.

You Will Be Saved *(Romans 10: 9-10)*

9. Because, if you confess with your lips

That Jesus is Lord for your worships,

And believe in your heart what he said,

Further **that God raised him from the dead,**

Then **you will be** forgiven and **saved**

And your past transgressions will be waived.

10. For the **man** who **believes with his heart**

And so is justified for his part,

And he then **confesses with his lips**

And so is saved from his thoughtless slips.

Renewal of Your Mind   *(Romans 12: 2)*

Do not be conformed to this earthly ***world*** you find

But be transformed by the renewal of your mind,

That you may prove what is the will of God effect**,**

What is good and acceptable and yes**,** ***perfect.***

Conduct   (Romans 12: 9-13)

9. Let love be genuine and unconditional;

Hate what is evil, bad or oppositional;

Hold fast to what is good as your first election;

10. Love one another with brotherly affection;

Outdo one another in showing honor, too.

11. Never flag or tire **in zeal** to be just and true,

Be aglow with the Spirit and keep your faith strong,

Serve the Lord every day and all the day long.

12. Rejoice in your hope, desire and expectation;

Be patient in all your trials and **tribulation,**

Be constant in prayer and consistent in restraints.

13. Contribute to the needs of the angels and ***saints,***

Practice sharing, giving and ***hospitality.***

Show humility and congeniality.

No Power But Of God   *(Romans 13: 1 (KJV))*

Let every soul be subject unto the higher powers

Of the sole governing authority in heaven's towers.

For there is no power but power received or gained ***of God:***

The powers that be are created by and ***ordained of God.***

Never Heard of Him   *(Romans 15: 21)*

"They shall see who have never been told a word of him,

And they shall understand who have never heard of him."

What God Has Prepared   *(1 Corinthians 2: 9)*

But, as it is** now **written,

No longer to be smitten,

***"What no eye has seen** received,*

        Nor ear** explicitly **heard,

Nor the heart of man conceived,

        Nor evoked in spoken word,

What God has** deftly **prepared,

And what is finally shared;

For his light now shines above dim

For** all of **those who love him."

Have Not Love   *(1 Corinthians 13: 1-3)*

1. *If I speak in the tongues of men and of angels* above,

But lack empathy, sensitivity and ***have not love,***

I am just ***a noisy gong or a*** loud ***clanging cymbal***,

A selfish soul as inconsequential as a thimble.

2. *And if I have prophetic powers* beyond all college,

And understand all mysteries and possess ***all knowledge,***

And if I have all faith and confidence that I believe,

So as to remove mountains, cause them to rise up and leave,

But have not love, I am nothing and my life has no worth.

3. *If I give away all I have* made and saved from my birth,

And even ***if I deliver my body to be burned,***

But have not love, I gain nothing from all that I have earned.

Love Never Ends *(1 Corinthians 13: 4-8)*

4. *Love is patient and kind;*

It is nascent and blind;

Love is not jealous or boastful,

Nor is it zealous, but hopeful;

5. *It is not arrogant or rude*

And is not indignant or crude.

Love does not insist on its own way,

Nor does it resist for its own say;

It is not irritable or resentful,

And is not irascible or revengeful;

6. *It does not rejoice at wrong,*

Nor does it enjoin the throng,

But rejoices in the right,

While conjoining in the light.

7. Love bears all things, believes all things,

Cares for all things, achieves all things,

Hopes for ***all things, endures all things***,

Copes with all things and cures all things**.**

8. For love transcends

And ***never ends.***

Childish Ways   *(1 Corinthians 13: 11)*

*When I was **just** a child,*

I spoke** just **like a child,

I thought** just **like a child,

I reasoned like a child;

When I became a man

My grownup life began,

I gave up childish ways

For the rest of my days.

Love Is the Greatest   *(1 Corinthians 13: 13)*

*So faith, hope, and **love abide**,*

And ***these three*** should be your guide;

But the greatest of these three

Is love shared unselfishly.

Death's Victory   *(1 Corinthians 15: 55)*

"O death, where is thy victory

To alter my trajectory*?*

O death, tell me ***where is thy sting***

To save me from sin and death's sling*?"*

In Christ   *(2 Corinthians 5: 17)*

Therefore, if any one is in Christ

His former life has been sacrificed,

And ***he is a*** brand ***new creation***,

Born again to joy and elation;

The old way of life ***has passed away,***

Behold, the new life ***has come*** to stay.

Benediction II   *(2 Corinthians 13: 14)*

May **the** saving ***grace of the Lord Jesus Christ***

And the love of God whose son he sacrificed,

And the fellowship of the Holy Spirit

Be with you all as you gratefully hear it**.**

One Word   (Galatians 5: 14)

For the whole law is fulfilled in just **one word,**

It is the most beautiful word ever heard,

"You shall love your neighbor as you love **yourself."**

Unselfish love should not be left on the shelf.

Sow to the Spirit   *(Galatians 6: 7-10)*

7. Please listen and ***do not be deceived*** or shocked;

God is steadfast and ***not*** ridiculed or ***mocked,***

For whatever a man sows and grows to keep***,***

That he will also harvest and store to ***reap.***

8. **For he who sows to his own flesh** and desires

Will from the flesh reap, and ***corruption*** transpires***;***

But he who sows to the Spirit avoids strife;

He ***will from the Spirit reap eternal life.***

9. And let us not grow weary in well-doing,

For in due season we shall reap, pursuing

Everything that is righteous, good and smart***,***

If we are diligent and ***do not lose heart.***

10. So then, as we have** the **opportunity,

***Let us do good to all men** for unity,*

***And especially to those** life achievers*

***Who are of the household of faith**'s believers.*

Christ Shall Give You Light *(Ephesians 5: 14)*

"Awake, O sleeper, and arise from the dead,

And Christ shall give you light"; believe what he said.

All Things Through Christ *(Phil. 4: 13 (KJV))*

I can do all things,

Give my heart its wings,

Through** Jesus, the **Christ

(Whom God sacrificed)

Which strengtheneth me

To glorify thee.

God's Beloved Son   *(Colossians 1: 15-20)*

15. He is the true *image of the invisible God,*

The first-born of all creation and God's lightning rod;

16. For in him all things were imagined and **created,**

In heaven and on earth just as God orchestrated**,**

Both **visible and invisible** by the millions**,**

Whether empires or kingdoms or **thrones or dominions**

Or principalities or authorities or rules –

All things were created through him and for him as tools**.**

17. He is before all things, including earth and weather**,**

And in him all things stay in tune and **hold together.**

18. *He is the head of the body, the church*'s headstone;

He is the beginning, who sits by God on his throne,

The first-born from the dead bringing God's new covenant,

That in everything he might be preeminent.

19. *For in him all the fullness of God was pleased to dwell,*

20. *And through him to reconcile to himself all things* quell,

Whether on earth or in heaven with nary a loss,

Making peace and harmony *by the blood of his cross.*

Coming of the Lord   *(1 Thessalonians 5: 2)*

For you yourselves know well as plumb

That the day of the Lord will come

In silence and hidden from sight

Like a cunning *thief in the night.*

Mystery of Our Religion   *(1 Timothy 3: 16)*

Great indeed, we confess but a smidgen*,*

Is the mystery of our religion:

He was manifested, born *in the flesh,*

Vindicated in the Spirit afresh*,*

Seen by angels, preached among the nations,

Believed on in the world's congregations*,*

Crucified on the cross in his story

And the third day *taken up in glory.*

God Is Good   *(1 Timothy 4: 4-5)*

4. For everything created by God is good,

And nothing is to be rejected by manhood

If it is gratefully *received with thanksgiving;*

5. For then it is consecrated for the living

By the word of God in dedication *and prayer*

For every child of God to enjoy and share.

Root of All Evils   (1 Timothy 6: 6-10)

6. *There is great gain in godliness with contentment* tightly furled;

7. *For* as all of God's children *we brought nothing into the world,*

And we cannot take anything out of the world when we leave;

8. *But if we have food and clothing* and give thanks when we receive,

With these needs satisfied *we shall be content* with our station.

9. *But those who desire to be rich* can *fall into temptation,*

Into a snare, into many senseless and hurtful desires

That plunge men into ruin and destruction playing with fires.

10. ***For the love of money is the root of all evils'*** decay;

It is through this craving and lust ***that some have wandered away***

From the faith and pierced their hearts with many pangs of sharp distress,

For the worship of wealth is not a recipe for success.

Spirit of Fear *(2 Timothy 1: 7 (KJV))*

For God hath not given us the spirit of fear;

The feeling of dread we needlessly hold so dear,

But of power, and of love, and of a sound mind

To leave apprehension, concern and fear behind.

Reminders *(Titus 3: 1-2)*

1. Remind them to be submissive to rulers and authorities,

To be truthful and trustworthy as their high priorities,

To be obedient, to be ready for any honest work,

Whether it be manual labor, menial or part time clerk,

2. To speak evil of no one, to avoid senseless **quarreling** then,

To be gentle, and to show perfect courtesy toward all men.

Mercy and Grace *(Titus 3: 5-7)*

5. *He saved us,* not because of our religiousness,

Not because of deeds done by us in righteousness,

But in virtue of his own mercy and station***,***

By the washing of sin to ***regeneration***,

Cleansing ***and renewal in the Holy Spirit,***

6. *Which he poured out upon us richly* to hear it

And share it ***through Jesus Christ our*** Lord and ***Savior***

To all of the nations as our new behavior***,***

7. *So that we might* all ***be justified by his grace***

And become heirs in hope of eternal life's place***.***

The Covenant   *(Hebrews 10: 16)*

"This is the covenant's new stem

That I will plant and *make with them*

After those dark *days, says the Lord:*

So all of them will get on board,

I will put my laws on their hearts,

And write them on their minds like charts*,"*

The Nature of Faith *(Hebrews 11: 1-3)*

1. Now faith is the assurance of things prayed about and **hoped for,**

The conviction of things not seen but imagined from days of yore.

2. For by it the men of old received their **divine approval.**

3. By faith we understand the importance of sin removal,

That the world was created by the word of God to revere,

So that what is seen was made out of things which do not appear.

Run With Perseverance   *(Hebrews 12: 1)*

Therefore, since we are completely *surrounded,*

Pursued, tormented and doggedly hounded

By so great a cloud of troubling *witnesses,*

Who suffer from their own chronic sicknesses,

Let us also lay aside every weight,

And sin which clings so closely to seal our fate,

And let us run with speed and *perseverance,*

Overcoming distractions and interference,

The race and challenge *that is set before us*,

To cleanse, reinvigorate and restore us.

Discipline of the Lord   *(Hebrews 12: 5-6)*

5. ..."My son, do not regard lightly the discipline of the Lord,

Nor lose courage when you are punished by him to be restored.

6. For the Lord disciplines him whom he loves and who believes,

And chastises every son or daughter *whom he receives."*

Strive For Peace *(Hebrews 12: 14)*

Strive for peace with all your fellow ***men,***

And for the holiness of love then,

Without which no one will see the Lord

And achieve their ultimate reward.

Faith Without Works   *(James 2: 14)*

What does it profit, my brethren with your quirks,

If a man says he has faith but has not works?

Can his faith alone *save him* without good deeds*?*

Faith is useless without action that fills needs.

Eyes and Face of the Lord   *(1 Peter 3: 10-12)*

10. For "He that would love life and see good days should feel joy and smile**,**

Let him keep his tongue from evil and his lips from speaking guile;

11. Let him turn away from everything **evil and do right,**

Let him seek peace and stubbornly **pursue it** with all his might**.**

12. For the eyes of the Lord are upon the righteous to take care**,**

And his ears are open and tuned in**to** receiving **their prayer.**

But the face of the Lord is against those that would **do evil,"**

For their lives are destined for a devastating upheaval.

A Thousand Years   *(2 Peter 3: 8-9)*

8. But do not** ever **ignore this one** single **fact,

Or give it reason, my ***beloved,*** to not act,

That with the Lord one day is as a thousand years,

And a thousand years as one day so it appears.

9. The Lord is not really ***slow about his promise***

As some would ***count slowness*** like a doubting Thomas,

But is forgiving and ***forbearing toward you,***

Not wishing that any should perish or fall through,

But that all should find their way and ***reach repentance,***

Releasing themselves from the pain of life's sentence.

Keep His Word *(1 John 2: 4-6)*

4. He who says "I know him" like a village crier

But disobeys his commandments is a liar,

And the truth is not in him as he inferred;

5. But whoever understands and *keeps his word,*

In him truly love for God is perfected

And his life will be joyously affected.

By this we may be sure of God's love and care

And *that we are in him* forever to share:

6. He who says he abides in him when he talked

Ought to walk in the same way in which he walked.

In the Light   *(1 John 2: 9-10)*

9. He who says he is in the light of God's will

And hates his brother is in the darkness still.

10. He who loves his brother abides in the light,

And in it there is no cause for stumbling spite.

No Fear in Love   *(1 John 4: 18)*

There is no fear in love, so it should not appear,

But perfect love casts out every hint of *fear.*

For fear has to do with punishment from above**,**

And he who fears is not yet *perfected in love.*

The Time is Near   *(Revelation 1: 3)*

Blessed is he who reads or shouts ***aloud***

The words of the prophecy in a crowd,

And blessed are those who hear and share in,

And all ***who keep what is written therein,***

For the time for final judgment ***is near***

And those who believe have nothing to fear.

Open the Door   (Revelation 3: 20)

***Behold, I stand** tirelessly **at the door and knock**,*

And I wait patiently for the door to unlock;

If anyone hears my voice and opens the door,

If one makes the choice who cannot cope anymore,

I will come in to him,

And** I will **eat with him,

There I will be,

And he with me.

King of the Ages   (Revelation 15: 3-4)

3. ..."***Great and wonderful are thy*** creations and ***deeds,***

O Lord God the Almighty who inspired our creeds***!***

Just and true are thy commandments and wondrous ***ways,***

O King of the ages deserving of high praise***!***

4. ***Who shall not fear***, honor ***and glorify the Lord?***

For thou alone art holy, righteous and adored.

All nations shall come and worship thee to be sealed,

For thy judgments have been sanctified and ***revealed."***

Death Shall Be No More   *(Revelation 21: 3-4)*

3. ..."Behold, the dwelling of God is with his women and his *men.*

He will dwell with them, and they shall be his people always then,

And God himself will be with them to nurture and supervise;

4. He will comfort and *wipe away every tear from their eyes,*

And destruction and *death shall be no more* to darken their door,

Neither shall there be mourning nor crying nor pain any more,

For the former things causing hurt and heartache *have passed away"*

And salvation in the presence of God will be there to stay.